Six-Word Lessons on Emotional Healing

100 Lessons to Navigate from Surviving to Thriving

Rae Ann Hall

Published by Pacelli Publishing
Bellevue, Washington

SIX ~WORD LESSONS

Six-Word Lessons on Emotional Healing

Cover and interior designed by Pacelli Publishing
Cover photo by Pixabay.com

Published by Pacelli Publishing
9905 Lake Washington Blvd. NE, #D-103
Bellevue, Washington 98004
PacelliPublishing.com

ISBN 10: 1-967256-05-5
ISBN-13: 978-1-967256-05-1

Dedication

For Kori, your bravery inspires me!

Contents

Introduction

As an adult survivor of adverse childhood experiences and narcissistic relationships, I've learned that healing continues throughout life—even in later years. Healing is not linear. It unfolds in layers, and as I progressed on my journey, it became clear that I needed to go deeper. I realized I had to be more intentional about my wellbeing, my choices, and the patterns that shaped my life.

There are long-term effects of abuse, and if we are not vigilant and proactive about healing, we can unconsciously sabotage ourselves by being drawn to unhealthy situations and people. To truly thrive, we must look beneath the surface and address the hidden wounds that create harmful patterns, limiting beliefs, and painful cycles.

I am a Certified Trauma-Informed Somatic Life Coach, a Certified Color Code Personality Trainer, and a Certified Laughter Yoga Teacher. These three certifications have been extraordinarily helpful in guiding my own healing journey and in supporting others to live with true mind-body-spirit synchronicity. In this book, I share practical tools and insights drawn from both my personal experience and my coaching practice.

This is not medical advice, but rather a resource to help you explore and understand what has been buried within. You'll find guidance on processing emotions, understanding how trauma affects the mind and body, and recognizing how attachment styles influence your relationships. You will learn to break trauma bonds, release stored pain through somatic practices, and tap into the transformative power of laughter.

Beyond healing, this book offers ways to strengthen your relationship with yourself, use mantras and affirmations to connect with your higher self, and embrace forgiveness as a path to freedom. My goal is to provide simple, meaningful, and practical tools that empower you to move forward with clarity, self-compassion, and joy.

These easy-to-absorb messages may support you on your healing path. Remember: life is meant to be enjoyed. Free yourself from what holds you back, so you can experience the best of what life offers and reach your full potential. Heal whatever created limiting beliefs. Reclaim your emotional freedom. Open the door to joy, fulfillment, self-love, acceptance, hope, optimism, and a vibrant present and future.

You deserve to thrive!

Rae Ann Hall
Certified Trauma-Informed Somatic Life Coach
Certified Laughter Yoga Teacher
Certified Color-Code Personality Trainer

Processing Feelings that Arise in You

1

Name the feeling you are feeling.

Name the feeling you're experiencing, because putting words to emotions like "I feel hurt," "I feel anxious," or "I feel dismissed" helps the brain shift from overwhelm to clarity. Even if you're unsure, guessing is okay and supports emotional regulation and understanding.

2

Allow the feeling without judging it.

Allow the feeling without judgment by replacing thoughts like “I shouldn’t feel this” with “This is what I’m feeling right now.” Acceptance doesn’t mean you like the emotion; it simply acknowledges your experience, fostering self-compassion and emotional clarity.

3

Slow down your body first. Breathe.

Slow down your body first, because emotions settle more easily in a regulated body. Try a slow exhale, stretching your shoulders, or placing a hand on your chest or stomach. A calmer body supports a calmer mind and emotional clarity.

4

Feeling is trying to tell you.

Emotions are messengers trying to communicate something important. Ask yourself, "What need isn't being met? What boundary was crossed? What part of me is hurting?" This approach transforms feelings into useful information, guiding self-understanding, problem-solving, and emotional healing.

5

Write out thoughts in your mind.

Journaling helps release spinning thoughts from your mind, creating clarity and emotional relief. Use prompts like "I am feeling...," "What triggered this?," and "What do I need right now?" to explore emotions, identify needs, and process experiences constructively.

6

Choose someone safe to talk to.

Sharing your feelings with the right person can lift emotional weight. A safe listener validates your experience, truly hears you, and avoids minimizing your emotions. This creates support, understanding, and connection that fosters healing, clarity, and emotional relief.

7

Use grounding techniques when you're overwhelmed.

When emotions feel overwhelming, use grounding techniques to stay present. Engage your senses using the 5-4-3-2-1 sensory check: notice 5 things you see, 4 you feel, 3 you hear, 2 you smell, 1 you taste. Touch textured objects or count breaths to calm and anchor yourself.

8

Separate the emotion from your identity.

Separate the emotion from your identity by shifting your language. Instead of saying, “I am anxious,” try, “I’m experiencing anxiety.” This distinction reminds you that feelings are temporary experiences moving through you, not defining who you are.

9

Give yourself permission to feel waves.

Give yourself permission to feel emotions in waves, understanding that you don't need to resolve everything at once. Processing occurs in layers, so it's okay to step away and return later, allowing feelings to be experienced and integrated gradually.

10

Small action of care for you.

Ask yourself, "What is one tiny act of care I can do right now?" It could be drinking water, taking a walk, playing calming music, or resting for five minutes. These small actions cultivate inner safety and self-nurturing.

Trauma's Stored in Mind and Body

11

Trauma gets stored as implicit memory.

Trauma often resides as implicit memory, showing up as reactions without clear words or images. You can practice journaling or voice notes to gradually put language to sensations and emotions. Naming these experiences helps reduce their intensity and promotes healing.

12

Trauma lives in the nervous system.

Trauma can live in the nervous system as hypervigilance, keeping your body on high alert even when danger has passed. Grounding techniques—like the 5-4-3-2-1 sensory check or holding something cold—help calm the sympathetic nervous system and restore balance.

13

Trauma causes reaction in the body.

Trauma often becomes stored in the body as muscle tension, commonly in the shoulders, jaw, or stomach. Gentle somatic practices like stretching, shaking out limbs, or slow neck and shoulder releases help to signal safety to your body and release stored tension.

14

Trauma disrupts your brain's time perception.

Trauma can distort your brain's sense of time, making past events feel like they are happening in the present. Remind yourself aloud, "That was then. This is now," to help reorient your mind and restore connection to the present moment.

15

Trauma can affect your breathing patterns.

Trauma can disrupt natural breathing patterns, often causing unconscious breath-holding. Practice box breathing: inhaling for four counts, holding four, exhaling four, and holding four. This helps regulate the breath, calm the nervous system and reduce stress, restoring balance and emotional stability.

16

Trauma can lead to emotional numbness.

Trauma can create emotional numbness as the mind shuts down feelings for protection. Reconnect with small, safe sensations like warm water, soft fabrics, or pleasant scents to gently awaken emotional circuits, restore awareness, and safely reengage with your feelings.

17

Trauma can often create looping thoughts.

Your brain often replays past scenarios, attempting to make sense of them. Practice “thought labeling” by saying, “This is a worry. This is a memory. This is a fear.” Creating this mental distance reduces overwhelm and supports emotional clarity and regulation.

18

Trauma triggers create fast emotional reactions.

Trauma triggers can provoke rapid emotional reactions, as your brain associates certain cues with danger. When triggered, practice orientation by looking around and naming five objects. This simple technique engages the rational brain, calming emotional intensity and promoting present-moment awareness.

19

Trauma can distort beliefs about yourself.

Trauma can distort beliefs about yourself, often creating shame, guilt, or feelings of unworthiness rooted in survival responses rather than truth. Practice gentle self-correction by saying, “This is a trauma belief, not a fact,” to separate your identity from trauma.

20

Trauma often makes you feel isolated.

Trauma often creates isolation, as the brain may perceive connection as unsafe. Build small, safe moments of connection—reaching out to a trusted friend, joining supportive groups, or spending time in shared spaces. Gradually, these experiences help rewire your sense of safety.

Understanding Your Attachment Style in Relationships

21

Understanding your attachment style helps you.

Know your attachment style as a map, not a label. Styles like secure, anxious, avoidant, or fearful-avoidant describe tendencies, not identity. Use this awareness to understand yourself better, guide growth, and foster healthier relationships without falling into self-blame.

22

Anxious attachment: fear of loss emotions

Anxious partners often overthink, seek reassurance, or fear abandonment. Practice self-soothing before reaching out by taking deep breaths, grounding yourself, or writing down your feelings. This helps you respond thoughtfully instead of reacting from anxiety, strengthening emotional regulation and confidence.

23

Avoidant attachment: Independence protects my vulnerability.

Avoidant partners may withdraw, downplay feelings, or shut down during conflict. Try sharing one small feeling or need early, which prevents emotional overwhelm later. This gentle practice builds connection, improves communication, and supports more secure, balanced relationship patterns.

24

Fearful-avoidant wants closeness, fears it.

Fearful-avoidant individuals crave closeness yet fear it, often fluctuating between seeking intimacy and pulling away due to past hurt. Focus on small, predictable routines with your partner, as consistency builds safety, reduces anxiety, and supports more secure connection over time.

25

Secure attachment: comfort, closeness and independence

Secure attachment balances closeness and independence, allowing partners to communicate needs clearly, repair conflict, and trust the connection. Even if you aren't naturally secure, you can learn secure behaviors over time; it's a skill set developed through practice and consistency.

26

Triggers reveal wounds; doesn't mean incompatibility.

Triggers don't indicate incompatibility, they reveal unresolved wounds. Attachment stress is normal and simply shows where healing is needed. Saying, "I'm feeling triggered, not attacked," helps prevent escalation, fosters understanding, and supports healthier communication during emotional moments.

27

Communication styles reflect an attachment pattern.

Communication styles often reflect attachment patterns: anxious partners pursue, avoidant partners withdraw, and secure partners discuss. Noticing your pattern in conflict and pausing before reacting can shift the entire outcome. A simple sixty-second pause fosters clarity, calm, and healthier communication.

28

Reparations matter more than perfection does.

Reparations matter more than perfection, because even healthy couples argue; what makes them secure is how they repair. Using phrases like "I understand now," "I want us to feel close again," or "Let me try that differently" strengthens connection and trust.

29

Self-regulation improves all attachment styles.

Self-regulation strengthens every attachment style, because most conflict happens when one or both people are emotionally dysregulated. Practice grounding, mindful breathing, or taking brief time-outs to return to calm before problem-solving. This creates clearer communication, reduces escalation, and supports healthier connections.

30

Change your attachment style through relationships.

Attachment patterns are not fixed; supportive relationships can gradually rewire the brain. Seek connections where you feel heard, respected, and emotionally safe. These experiences strengthen trust, reduce old attachment fears, and help you develop more secure patterns over time.

Healing and Releasing a Trauma Bond

31

Trauma bond is an emotional attachment.

A trauma bond is an intense, addictive emotional attachment formed between two people when there is a cycle of intermittent reinforcement. This is defined by periods of affection, validation, or closeness mixed with periods of pain, fear, manipulation, neglect, or inconsistency.

32

Stop romanticizing good moments and highs.

The “good moments” in a trauma bond often feel intense, but they come from relief after pain. They are not proof of a healthy relationship. When romanticizing the good moments, it is important to remind yourself that the highs do not outweigh the harm.

33

Limit or cut contact when possible.

Distance weakens the chemical loop of dopamine and cortisol that sustains trauma bonds. Even reducing the frequency of communication allows your nervous system to stabilize, promoting emotional clarity, self-regulation, and healthier boundaries.

34

Create counter list of painful moments.

Your brain will try to only remember the good. Create a counter list of painful moments to counteract trauma bonding, which often selectively filters memory. Writing down harmful actions helps your brain acknowledge reality, maintain clarity, and resist idealizing the relationship, supporting emotional awareness and healthier decision-making.

35

Strengthen self-worth through daily acts.

Strengthen your self-worth through daily acts, because trauma bonds thrive on insecurity. Each day, do one thing that affirms, "I take care of me." Consistently nurturing yourself builds internal safety, reinforces confidence, and reduces the influence of unhealthy attachments.

36

Reconnect with safe people, healthy relationships.

Healthy relationships help regulate your nervous system. Spend time with people who are consistent, supportive, and calming, allowing your body to experience safety. These connections foster emotional stability, reduce stress, and reinforce a sense of security, trust, and wellbeing.

37

Understand what the biological addiction is.

Understand the biological nature of trauma bonds, which trigger dopamine, cortisol, and oxytocin in unstable patterns. Recognizing that you're not "crazy" helps you break this chemical cycle. Approach yourself with compassion, supporting healing and emotional clarity through awareness and self-care.

38

Learn your attachment triggers with curiosity.

Learn your attachment triggers with curiosity by asking questions like, "Do I fear abandonment?" or "Do I shut down to avoid vulnerability?" Understanding these triggers diminishes the power of the bond, increases self-awareness, and supports healthier emotional responses and relationships.

39

Turn focus on your future identity.

Focus on your future identity by envisioning who you are becoming after this bond. Visualizing a healthier, stronger version of yourself creates psychological distance from the relationship, fosters personal growth, and empowers you to make choices aligned with your wellbeing and self-respect.

40

Replace trauma bond with self-bond.

Healing begins by forming a secure attachment with yourself through regular routines, emotional check-ins, self-validation, and gentle boundaries. Strengthening this self-bond reduces the power of trauma bonds, fosters emotional resilience, and cultivates a sense of safety, stability, and self-trust.

Healing Deeper Wounds and Your Strongholds

41

Identify root belief behind the wound.

Deep wounds often form core beliefs such as “I’m not enough,” “I’m unlovable,” or “People always leave.” To heal, write the wound, identify the belief, and then create a gentler truth, like reframing “I’m unlovable” as learned pain, not fact.

42

Feel emotion instead of the story.

To heal, feel the emotion itself rather than the story behind it, because strongholds are reinforced by repeating mental narratives. Sit with the sensation, notice where it resides in your body, and explore its message to release the stored energy.

43

Inner reparenting helps increase self-love.

Practice inner reparenting to cultivate self-love, addressing wounds rooted in past lack of protection, validation, or comfort. Speak to yourself with care: “I hear you,” “You’re safe with me,” “I won’t abandon you.” This creates internal safety that gently unwinds old patterns.

44

Break the cycle of self-abandonment.

Break the cycle of self-abandonment, which often stems from deep wounds causing ignored needs. Each day, ask yourself, “What do I need right now?” and consciously meet that need, even in small ways, fostering self-care, healing, and emotional resilience.

45

Release the body's memory of wound.

Your nervous system physically stores emotional pain, creating tension and strongholds. Healing tools such as shaking out limbs, gentle stretching, humming, deep exhaling, or grounding your hands in warm water facilitate somatic release, helping to release stored energy and restore balance.

46

Use corrective emotional experiences for healing.

Your wounds stem from unsafe experiences, but healing arises from safe ones. Allow people to show up for you and let yourself be seen in small ways, giving your nervous system the opportunity to learn, "This time, it's different."

47

Replace harsh inner dialogue with truth.

Deep wounds often speak like inner critics, but responding with truth-centered language promotes healing. When self-attacks arise, say, "That's an old fear speaking," or "My worth is not up for debate." Repeating this practice gradually rewires thought patterns and strengthens self-worth.

48

Challenge the stronghold. Use micro-boundaries.

Strongholds often develop from people-pleasing, avoidance, or over-giving. To heal, practice one small boundary each day, such as saying “no,” pausing before replying, or expressing a preference. These tiny boundaries gradually weaken deep wounds and strengthen self-respect.

49

Create meaning from pain, not identity.

Healing doesn't mean forgetting; it means integrating your experiences. Reflect on questions like, "What strength, intuition, or wisdom grew from this wound?" This allows you to uncover lessons without letting the wound define your identity, fostering growth and resilience.

50

Build future self without the wound.

Build a future self who no longer operates from old wounds. Deep wounds lose power when you move from past-based living to purpose-based living. Visualize a grounded, confident, safe version of yourself and take one small daily action that aligns with it.

Somatic Practices to Release Stored Pain

51

Neurogenic tremors and therapeutic shaking practices

Neurogenic tremors and therapeutic shaking mimic how animals release stress naturally. Stand or sit and gently shake your hands, arms, legs, and whole body for thirty to sixty seconds. This practice helps discharge stuck survival energy from fight-or-flight responses, promoting relaxation and emotional release.

52

Using deep exhaling to release pain.

Deep exhaling helps release emotional pain, which often appears as breath-holding. Inhale normally, then exhale very slowly through the mouth like a sigh, repeating five to ten times. Long exhales activate the parasympathetic system, promoting calm, relaxation, and emotional relief.

53

Heart and chest opening stretch exercise

The heart and chest opening stretch helps release stored sadness and grief. Sit or stand tall, roll your shoulders back, and gently lift your chest while taking slow breaths into the sternum. This practice eases emotional tightness and promotes relaxation.

54

Vagus nerve stimulation: humming and vibration

Vagus nerve stimulation through humming supports emotional regulation. On each exhale, hum low and steady, allowing vibrations to resonate through your throat and chest. This practice relaxes the nervous system, promotes calm, and enhances emotional balance and overall wellbeing.

55

Butterfly hug (bilateral tapping) for grounding

The butterfly hug, or bilateral tapping, supports grounding during overwhelming emotions. Cross your arms over your chest and tap your shoulders alternately left and right. This technique helps process emotions, soothe the body, and promote nervous system regulation and calm.

56

Body scanning and naming sensations practice

Body scanning and naming sensations transforms vague discomfort into present-moment awareness. Close your eyes and scan from feet to head, labeling feelings as "tight," "warm," "fluttery," or "pressure." Naming these sensations helps discharge their intensity and fosters nervous system regulation.

57

Grounding through the feet when overwhelmed

Grounding through the feet helps when feeling overwhelmed or disconnected. Stand or sit with your feet on the floor, imagining your weight sinking into the earth. This practice calms the lower body, signals safety to the nervous system, and promotes stability.

58

Self-soothing touch helps nervous system.

Self-soothing touch helps regulate your nervous system by communicating safety and comfort. Place one hand on your heart and one on your belly while breathing slowly. Warm, gentle touch signals reassurance to the body, promoting calm, emotional regulation, and healing.

59

Psoas release exercise (leg drop stretch)

The psoas muscle stores fear and stress and releasing it supports emotional and physical wellbeing. Lie on your back with knees bent, gently letting them fall to each side. Soft, slow movement helps release core tension and restore balance.

60

Use orienting practice (look around slowly).

Use the orienting practice by slowly turning your head and observing your surroundings, noticing colors, shapes, and objects. This technique helps release hypervigilance and signals your nervous system that you are safe, promoting calm, presence, and emotional regulation.

Laughter Heals, Calms, and Is Healthy

61

Reduces stress hormones and lowers cortisol

Laughter lowers cortisol and adrenaline, helping your body shift from fight-or-flight into a state of relaxation. This natural release reduces stress, promotes healing, and supports overall wellbeing, showing how something as simple as laughing can profoundly benefit both mind and body.

62

Boosts endorphins, is natural mood lifter

Laughing releases endorphins, your brain's natural "feel-good" chemicals, which help ease emotional pain and elevate mood. This simple act promotes mental and emotional healing, reduces stress, and encourages a sense of joy and wellbeing that supports overall health.

63

Relaxes muscle tension in your body.

A big laugh contracts and then releases muscles throughout your body, creating a natural tension–release cycle. This process softens physical tightness stored from stress, promoting relaxation, easing discomfort, and supporting both emotional and physical healing in a simple, effective way.

64

Activates parasympathetic nervous system, restores balance

Laughter activates the parasympathetic nervous system, shifting your body into "rest and digest" mode. This helps regulate the nervous system, restore balance, reduce stress, and promote relaxation, supporting both emotional stability and overall physical and mental wellbeing naturally.

65

Strengthens immune function in your body

Laughter strengthens immune function by increasing immune cells and antibodies, enhancing the body's natural defenses. This boost supports resilience, promotes overall wellbeing, and helps the body better respond to stress and illness, making laughter a simple yet powerful tool for health.

66

Improves oxygen flow: heart, lungs, brain

Laughing increases oxygen intake and stimulates the heart and lungs, acting like a mini workout for your body. This boosts oxygen flow to tissues and the brain, enhancing energy, alertness, and overall physical and mental wellbeing in a natural, enjoyable way.

67

Enhances social bonding and creates connection

Laughing with others fosters connection, safety, and a sense of belonging. This shared joy deeply regulates emotions, reduces stress and emotional distress, and strengthens social bonds, supporting mental health, resilience, and overall wellbeing through the powerful effects of positive social interaction.

68

Breaks rumination loops, interrupts negative thoughts

Laughter interrupts negative thought cycles and overthinking, providing the brain with a valuable "pattern break." This shift can alter your emotional state, reduce rumination, and promote a lighter, more positive mindset, supporting both mental clarity and emotional wellbeing.

69

Releases physical pain and reduces discomfort

Endorphins, released during laughter, act as natural painkillers, helping to temporarily reduce physical discomfort. This natural relief enhances overall wellbeing, supports the body's healing processes, and creates a sense of ease and comfort, making laughter a simple yet powerful therapeutic tool.

70

Improves emotional resilience in difficult situations

Laughing during difficult times shows the brain that joy remains accessible, even amid challenges. This practice builds psychological flexibility, fosters hope, strengthens inner resilience, and supports emotional recovery, helping you navigate hardships with greater strength, balance, and a positive outlook.

Relationship with Yourself and Your Worth

71

Treat yourself how you treat others.

Treat yourself with the same kindness you offer loved ones, because most people are gentler with others than themselves. When you make a mistake, ask, “What would I say to someone I care about?” and then speak that compassion to yourself.

72

Start keeping small promises to yourself.

Start keeping small promises to yourself, because self-worth grows from self-trust. Begin with tiny actions like drinking a glass of water, making your bed, or walking for three minutes. Consistency matters more than intensity, building reliability and confidence over time.

73

Stop abandoning yourself to please others.

Stop abandoning yourself to keep others comfortable, because silencing your needs weakens self-worth. Each day, ask yourself, “What do I need right now?” and honor that need in a small way. Prioritizing yourself strengthens confidence, balance, and emotional resilience.

74

Heal the inner critic in you.

Heal your inner critic by speaking to yourself in your own voice, not the critic's. This voice often echoes old wounds, not truth. When self-attack arises, remind yourself, "That's a past voice. What do I choose to believe?"

75

Build and implement "self-worth routine" daily.

Build a "self-worth routine" instead of waiting to feel better, because self-worth grows through repetition. Practices like a morning check-in, gentle movement, five minutes of stillness, and gratitude for yourself cultivate consistent self-respect, confidence, and emotional resilience every day.

76

Create boundaries that show you matter.

Boundaries protect your emotional space and wellbeing. Start with micro-boundaries like “I’ll reply later,” “I’m not available tonight,” or “I prefer this.” Practicing small boundaries consistently builds confidence, strengthens self-respect, and empowers you to maintain healthier, more balanced relationships over time.

77

Celebrate small wins like they matter.

Celebrate small wins because they truly matter—your brain remembers what you acknowledge. Each night, list three things you did well, even if they seem minor. Recognizing these achievements nurtures confidence, motivation, and a positive mindset, reinforcing your sense of progress daily.

78

Replace comparison with compassion for self.

Comparison undermines self-worth and steals joy. When you catch yourself measuring your journey against someone else's, remind yourself: "Their path is theirs. Mine is mine." This mindset nurtures self-acceptance, gratitude, and confidence in your unique experiences and growth.

79

Important to create joy and play.

It's important to create space for joy and play, not just focus on productivity. Allowing yourself to enjoy life teaches your nervous system that you are worthy of good things. Practice doing one activity each day purely for joy.

80

Visualize future self, and act accordingly.

Visualize your future self and make choices that honor them. Ask: "What would the version of me who loves themselves choose right now?" Then choose one small action aligned with that version. Self-worth grows when you treat yourself like someone valuable—consistently.

Mantras and Affirmations to Propel Forward

81

Mantras and affirmations defined with purpose

Mantra: A word, phrase, or sound repeated intentionally, often in meditation, prayer, or mindfulness practices. The purpose is to calm the mind, shift energy, and align your thoughts with higher intentions.

Affirmation: A positive statement that reflects a desired belief or reality. The purpose is to reprogram limiting beliefs, boost confidence, and strengthen a mindset of possibility.

82

How to use mantras and affirmations

Mantra Practice: Repeat these during meditation, journaling, or quietly throughout your day to align with self-love energy.

Affirmation Practice: Write these affirmations daily, place sticky notes around your space, or repeat them aloud in the mirror.

83

Mantras for forward momentum

"I am open and ready to receive all the abundance the universe offers me."

"I release what no longer serves me and make space for prosperity."

"Opportunities flow effortlessly into my life every day."

"I am aligned with my highest purpose and my dreams are manifesting."

"I trust the timing of my life and welcome success in every area.

84

Affirmations to manifest abundance in life

"I am worthy of all the good things life has to offer."

"I attract wealth, love, and joy effortlessly."

"Every day I grow stronger, wiser, and more confident."

"I am the creator of my reality, and I choose abundance now."

"I am grateful for all I have and all that is coming to me."

85

Mantras for increasing your self-love

"I am worthy of love and kindness, especially from myself."

"I honor my feelings, my body, and my spirit."

"I am whole, complete, and enough exactly as I am."

"I forgive myself and release the need for self-judgment."

"I nurture myself with compassion, patience, and care."

86

Affirmations for increasing your self-love

"I deeply accept and love myself for who I am."

"I deserve happiness, peace, and joy in my life."

"I treat myself with the same kindness I offer others."

"I trust myself and honor my inner guidance."

"I release shame and embrace my unique beauty and value.

87

Mantras for healing traumas causing pain

“I am safe in this moment, and my body is allowed to heal.”

“I release what no longer serves me and reclaim my power.”

“It is okay to feel, it is okay to let go.”

“I honor my journey and the courage it takes to heal.”

“I am whole, I am healing, I am enough.”

88

Affirmations for painful traumas

"I am safe, I am supported, and I am healing every day."

"I release the past and allow myself to live fully in the present."

"My pain does not define me; I am resilient and strong."

"I honor my feelings and give myself permission to feel and heal."

"With each breath, I reclaim my power, my peace, and my joy."

89

Mantras for joy. success in life

"I am worthy of joy, success, and all the blessings life has to offer."

"Every day I grow, thrive, and move closer to my goals."

"I attract opportunities, positivity, and success effortlessly."

"I choose happiness, gratitude, and joy in every moment."

"I am confident, capable, and deserving of all my dreams."

90

Affirmations for joy, success in life

"I deserve happiness, success, and fulfillment in every area of my life."

"I am confident, capable, and open to opportunities that bring me joy and growth."

"Each day I create experiences that bring me happiness and progress toward my goals."

"I release fear and embrace joy, abundance, and success in all forms."

"I attract joy, prosperity, and meaningful connections effortlessly."

How Forgiveness Can Set You Free

91

Understand purpose of forgiveness for you.

Forgiveness is an act of personal healing, not a gift to the other person. When you hold grudges, you keep yourself emotionally and physically tied to the pain, allowing past harm to influence your present wellbeing and limit your inner peace.

92

Acknowledge your feelings without suppressing them.

Before forgiving, allow yourself to fully experience emotions like anger, sadness, or betrayal. Giving these feelings space is essential, because ignoring or suppressing them only delays healing and prevents you from processing the hurt in a healthy, meaningful way today.

93

Recognize that forgiveness is a process.

Recognize that forgiveness is a gradual process that rarely happens overnight. Be patient and compassionate with yourself as you navigate the layers of emotion involved. Allowing time and gentle self-understanding helps you move forward with greater clarity, strength, and emotional freedom.

94

Forgiving yourself is key in healing.

Forgiving yourself is essential to healing because many people carry guilt or shame long after difficult experiences. Self-forgiveness matters as much as forgiving others. Releasing self-blame and accepting your own humanity allows you to grow, recover, and move forward today.

95

Shifting your perspective helps gain clarity.

Shifting your perspective can help you gain clarity by recognizing that everyone, including yourself, is doing the best they can with the awareness they have. This understanding doesn't excuse harmful actions, but it can ease emotional intensity and support healing.

96

Setting healthy boundaries is your right.

Setting healthy boundaries is your right, because forgiveness never requires reconciliation or continued exposure to harmful behavior. You can forgive someone while still protecting your wellbeing, choosing distance, and honoring what you need to feel safe and supported fully.

97

Writing or journaling can release feelings.

Writing or journaling can help release built-up feelings by giving your emotions a safe place to land. Writing a letter, even if you never send it, allows you to express hurt honestly and create clear statements of release and healing.

98

Combine forgiveness with mindfulness or meditation.

Combine forgiveness with mindfulness or meditation by visualizing yourself releasing emotional burdens. Imagine breathing out pain and breathing in peace, compassion, and calm. This simple practice supports emotional clarity, eases tension, and strengthens your ability to let go each day.

99

Practice empathy, not at your expense.

Practicing empathy can support healing by helping you understand why someone acted a certain way, but it should never come at your expense. Use empathy to gain insight, not to excuse abuse or allow mistreatment to continue in your life.

100

Notice the freedom it brings you.

Forgiveness lightens your emotional load, improves mental health, and reduces stress, while also supporting physical wellbeing. By letting go of past hurts, you free yourself from being a prisoner of the past, creating space for peace, clarity, and growth.

Resources

Manuela Mischke-Reeds, MA, LMFT, *Somatic Physiotherapy Toolbox* (Eu Claire, WI: PESI Publishing & Media, 2018)

Amir Levine, MD and Rachel S.F. Heller, MA, *Attached: The New Science of Adult Attachment and How It Can Help You Find—and Keep—Love* (New York: Penguin Random House, 2011)

Madan Kataria, MD, *Laughter Yoga: Daily Practices for Health and Happiness* (New York: Penguin Books, 2020)

Jeffrey Briar, *The Laughter Yoga Book* (Laguna Beach, CA: Creative Arts Press and The Laughter Yoga Institute, 2016)

About the Six-Word Lessons Series

Legend has it that Ernest Hemingway was challenged to write a story using only six words. He responded with the story, "For sale: baby shoes, never worn." The story tickles the imagination. Why were the shoes never worn? The answers are left up to the reader's imagination.

This style of writing has a number of aliases: postcard fiction, flash fiction, and micro-fiction. Lonnie Pacelli was introduced to this concept in 2009 by a friend, and started thinking about how this extreme brevity could apply to today's communication culture of text messages, tweets and Facebook posts. He wrote the first book, *Six-Word Lessons for Project Managers*, then he and his wife Patty started helping other authors write and publish their own books in the series.

The books all have six-word chapters with six-word lesson titles, each followed by a one-page description. They can be written by entrepreneurs who want to promote their businesses, or anyone with a message to share.

www.ingramcontent.com/pod-product-compliance
Lightning Source LLC
Chambersburg PA
CBHW071351230926
51846CB00002B/511
* 9 7 8 1 9 6 7 2 5 6 0 5 1 *